A CAPTAIN BEFORE HE WAS 21, a household name throughout most of Europe at 39 and killed in action just three weeks after his 47th birthday, Nelson lived a colourful and crowded life. As well as winning some of the most resounding victories in British history at the Nile (1798), Copenhagen (1801) and Trafalgar (1805) – and losing an arm and the sight of an eye in the process – he also had a tempestuous and very public love affair with Emma Hamilton, one of the most beautiful women of his day.

Affectionate, engaging and a devoted friend and father, he was also ruthless and occasionally even cruel. Uninspiring and unheroic in his personal appearance, he was also one of the most charismatic leaders Britain has ever produced, able to inspire devotion, even love, in those who served with him.

ABOVE: *A modern figure of Nelson based on the latest research into his appearance.*

It is this combination of opposites that makes him so fascinating and, as a result, there always seems to be something new to be said about him, some new insight into his complex character. Moreover, recent research has thrown fresh light on his battles and on his key relationships and, as a result, a new narrative of his life and career is beginning to emerge. Based on all the new material, this book offers a brief introduction to the story of the man who is still widely regarded as one of Britain's greatest heroes.

The Battle of Trafalgar *by W.L. Wyllie, with Nelson's flagship HMS* Victory *(left) at the height of the action.*

The Boy
1758–1779

ABOVE: *Nelson's signature as a young lieutenant.*

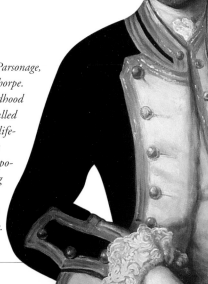

ABOVE: *Revd Edmund Nelson and Catherine Nelson. Both Nelson's parents were livelier than these rather stiff, formal portraits suggest.*

HORATIO NELSON WAS BORN on 29 September 1758 in the small village of Burnham Thorpe on the north coast of Norfolk. The son of the parish priest, Edmund Nelson, and his wife Catherine, he was a bright, engaging little boy who constantly sought attention and approval from adults and was naturally impulsive, especially in his affections. These two strands run right through his life and provide the underlying pattern to all his actions, public as well as private.

He did not have a conventional childhood. His mother died when he was nine – a psychological blow which left a permanent scar. Then, in March 1771, aged only 12, he joined the Royal Navy under the patronage of his uncle, Captain Maurice Suckling, and was away from home for most of his teens.

Even in the Navy his training was unconventional. Captain Suckling seems to have deliberately planned for the young Horatio to have as wide a variety of experience as possible. After a short spell in the Thames estuary in his uncle's ship, the 64-gun HMS *Raisonnable*, he made a voyage to the West Indies in the merchantman *Mary Ann*. Then, still aged only 14, he took part in an expedition to the Arctic and finally completed his early training with a two-year stint in the crack frigate HMS *Seahorse* in the East Indies, during which he saw action for the first time.

He then fell dangerously ill with malaria and had to be invalided home in 1775. Even so, his first four years in the Navy had been packed with activity and had given him a wide range of experience, in different types of ship and different environments, which helped to nurture his natural independence and energy.

LEFT: *The Parsonage, Burnham Thorpe. Nelson's childhood home was pulled down in his lifetime but this near-contemporary painting gives a good idea of what it looked like.*

ABOVE: *Nelson and the polar bear. This highly romanticized painting by Richard Westall depicts a famous incident during the expedition to the Arctic in 1773.*

Having recovered from his illness, Nelson passed his lieutenant's examination on 5 April 1777. After only a year in the frigate HMS *Lowestoffe* on the West Indies station, her captain, William Locker, gave him command of a small schooner that acted as the frigate's tender. Less than a year later, he was promoted to commander and was given his first independent command, the brig HMS *Badger*, and six months later, in June 1779, he received the key promotion to post captain, when he was still just three months short of his 21st birthday. Promotion this rapid was not as unusual as some have suggested in the past, but it was nonetheless impressive.

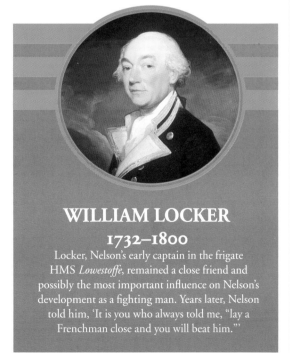

LEFT: *Captain Maurice Suckling, Nelson's maternal uncle, with whom he first went to sea in HMS* Raisonnable *in 1771.*

WILLIAM LOCKER

1732–1800

Locker, Nelson's early captain in the frigate HMS *Lowestoffe*, remained a close friend and possibly the most important influence on Nelson's development as a fighting man. Years later, Nelson told him, 'It is you who always told me, "lay a Frenchman close and you will beat him."'

Frigate Captain
1780–1793

FOLLOWING HIS PROMOTION, NELSON spent eight years almost continuously in command of frigates: the *Hinchinbrooke*, the *Albemarle* and finally the *Boreas*. For the early part of this period, Britain was at war with America and was also fighting the French and Spanish, who entered the war on the American side. So there were a number of major fleet actions and most of Nelson's contemporaries served in the battle squadrons. Nelson, by contrast, took part in only one action in 1780, when he was involved in the small-scale river-borne attack on the Spanish Fort San Juan in Nicaragua, following which he suffered a second bout of sickness which kept him out of active service for almost a year.

At this point, his career faltered and almost ended. A peacetime appointment in command of the frigate HMS *Boreas* in the West Indies between 1784 and 1787 was not happy. He became involved in a dispute over illicit trading between the colonies and the newly-independent American states, thus creating powerful enemies among the rich British traders and senior officials in the area. He also mishandled a delicate situation involving a son of King George III, Prince William Henry serving in the Navy in command of the frigate HMS *Pegasus*. When the Prince had a disagreement with his first lieutenant, William Schomberg, Nelson failed to defuse the potentially embarrassing incident and allowed the Prince to flout naval rules, thus earning the displeasure of the Admiralty and, indeed, of the king himself. So, between 1788 and 1793 he was unable to get any employment, despite repeated requests.

In the meantime, on 11 March 1787, he had married Frances (Fanny) Nisbet, a pretty and delightful young widow whom he had met on the island of Nevis.

Their courtship was warm and affectionate but the marriage was severely tested in its early years when they returned to Burnham Thorpe to live with Nelson's father. Unable to obtain another appointment in the Navy, Nelson became frustrated and irritable, while Fanny, used to the warm climate and relative luxury of the West Indies, had to adjust to genteel poverty in the icy winters of Norfolk. Also, as the years dragged by, it became clear that there were not to be any children. Fanny already had a son by her first marriage, Josiah Nisbet, but Nelson, who loved children, longed for some of his own.

RIGHT: *Captain Horatio Nelson, 1780, by Francis Rigaud. Nelson wears his new captain's uniform.*

NELSON'S HEIGHT

Nelson is often described as an unusually small man. Modern research has established that he was in fact about 5ft 6in/5ft 7in tall (1.7/1.8 metres), about the average for a man of his time.

ABOVE: *Nelson's mature right-handed signature, c.1785.*

FRANCES, LADY NELSON
1761–1831

Frances has often been portrayed as a cold, rather colourless woman who failed to support her brilliant husband. But as late as 1797 Nelson told a friend she was 'beautiful, accomplished, but above all that her angelic tenderness towards him was beyond imagination.' In fact, she was the innocent victim of Nelson's affair with Emma Hamilton that was extremely destructive as well as passionate and romantic. Fanny survived him by 30 years, always remaining devoted to his memory, even destroying some of his cruel letters to her, so as to protect his reputation for posterity.

BELOW: *HMS* Boreas *off St Eustatius in the West Indies, c.1785. Nelson's frigate in watercolour by Nicolas Pocock.*

Battleship Captain
1793–1796

IN EARLY 1793 WAR broke out with Revolutionary France and Nelson was offered command of the 64-gun battleship HMS *Agamemnon*. Having gathered a ship's company, including a largely hand-picked contingent from Norfolk, he sailed in her to join the Mediterranean fleet, under Admiral Lord Hood.

In 1794, Hood placed him in command of naval forces ashore during the capture of the island of Corsica and he was present at the siege and capture of two key towns: first Bastia, and then Calvi, where he was hit in the face by gravel thrown up from a parapet by a French cannonball. As a result, he lost almost all sight in his right eye and thereafter was only able to distinguish light from dark with it.

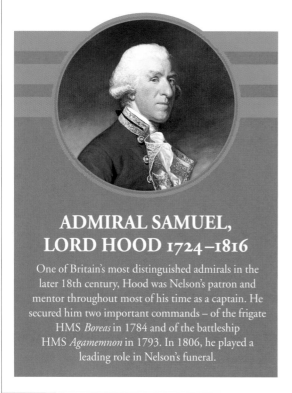

ADMIRAL SAMUEL, LORD HOOD 1724–1816

One of Britain's most distinguished admirals in the later 18th century, Hood was Nelson's patron and mentor throughout most of his time as a captain. He secured him two important commands – of the frigate HMS *Boreas* in 1784 and of the battleship HMS *Agamemnon* in 1793. In 1806, he played a leading role in Nelson's funeral.

ABOVE: *HMS* Agamemnon *(right) in action with the* Ça Ira *at the Battle of the Gulf of Genoa, March 1795. A watercolour by Nicholas Pocock.*

In 1795, he had a brief spell with the main fleet, by then commanded by Admiral William Hotham, during which time he took part in two fleet battles – the first of his career. At the Battle of the Gulf of Genoa (13/14 March 1795) he showed his independent approach by taking the *Agamemnon* to attack a disabled French ship the *Ça Ira*. He dealt the much larger ship and her crew such a heavy blow that she fell an easy prey to the British when the fighting resumed the next day. But he was furious when Hotham ended the action when only two prizes had been taken. He was then detached to Italy as a commodore in command of a small squadron, where he assisted the Austrian army in its fight against the victorious French armies under the rising new general Napoleon Bonaparte. He instituted a tight blockade of French-held ports, and organized the capture of the islands of Elba and Capraia in 1796. He also found time to court his first mistress, the opera singer Adelaide Correglia, whom he met in Leghorn.

This was an important stage in his career. It gave him experience of independent command, in which he took important operational decisions himself. Moreover, his exploits won him the regard of a number of influential people – notably the First Lord of the Admiralty, Lord Spencer, and the new commander-in-chief in the Mediterranean, Sir John Jervis. But, despite the approval of such men, he began to feel that he was not sufficiently appreciated back home in Britain. His letters to his wife and family at this time are full of complaints that his actions had not been publicly recognized or rewarded. But his fortunes were about to change.

LEFT: *Nelson at the siege of Calvi, 12 July 1794. A pen-and-wash drawing by William Bromley shows the moment when Nelson was struck in the face by gravel thrown up by a French round shot.*

The Battle of Cape St Vincent
14 FEBRUARY 1797

ABOVE: *Commodore Horatio Nelson (centre) leads his boarding party onto the deck of the Spanish three-decked battleship* San José. *Painting by George Jones.*

EARLY IN 1797 FRANCE and her allies planned a major invasion of British-held Ireland, backed by their fleets. But the opening moves were thwarted by Sir Admiral John Jervis's remarkable victory over the Spanish fleet at the Battle of Cape St Vincent, in which Nelson played a decisive role.

Past accounts of the battle have tended to portray Nelson as a lone genius who saved the day for the British by his unconventional approach. Modern research has revealed a much more complex picture. It is now clear that Jervis himself handled the battle unconventionally right from the outset. First he formed his ships into a loose line of battle and drove

swiftly for a gap in the Spanish line. Then, having split the enemy fleet into two unequal groups, he ordered his own fleet to attack the larger group in three divisions.

Nelson was a key player in this second phase of the battle. Noticing that his divisional flagship, the *Britannia*, was not obeying Jervis's signals, he took his ship, HMS *Captain*, out of the line and sailed directly to assist the leading British ships, which had by then

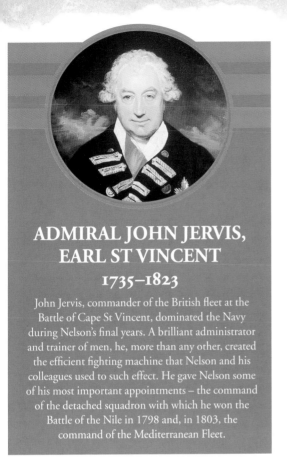

ADMIRAL JOHN JERVIS, EARL ST VINCENT
1735–1823

John Jervis, commander of the British fleet at the Battle of Cape St Vincent, dominated the Navy during Nelson's final years. A brilliant administrator and trainer of men, he, more than any other, created the efficient fighting machine that Nelson and his colleagues used to such effect. He gave Nelson some of his most important appointments – the command of the detached squadron with which he won the Battle of the Nile in 1798 and, in 1803, the command of the Mediterranean Fleet.

begun to catch up with the rearmost Spaniards. In the past, this unexpected manoeuvre has been described as an act of disobedience that could have cost him his career but it is now clear that he was acting in accordance with Jervis's intentions.

A fierce melée ensued, in which a number of Spanish ships suffered badly from the fast and accurate British broadsides. Two of them, the *San Nicolas* and the *San José*, while trying desperately to get out of range, collided and became entangled. Seeing this, Nelson ordered the *Captain* to be placed alongside the *San Nicolas* and then personally led a boarding party to capture her. The *San José*, which had already been badly mauled by gunfire from other British ships, began firing on Nelson and his party in an attempt to help their comrades. So he led his men up her sides and captured her as well. He thus was personally responsible for capturing two of the four prizes that were taken on that day.

It was a remarkable feat, unprecedented in naval history, and Nelson was deservedly the hero of the hour. He received a gold medal from the king and was made a Knight of the Bath, with the right to wear a distinctive star on his uniform coat and to style himself 'Sir Horatio Nelson'. The public recognition he had craved was his at last.

BELOW: *The bell of the* San José. *Nelson's prize was taken into the Royal Navy as HMS* San Josef. *When the ship was finally broken up many items were saved from her, including this bell.*

ABOVE: *Commodore Nelson receives the sword of the dying Spanish Admiral Winthuysen. Daniel Orme's engraving is a sanitized version of the scene – Nelson's uniform was in tatters and his face blackened with smoke.*

Santa Cruz de Tenerife

JULY 1797

NELSON'S SUCCESS AT Cape St Vincent was followed by one of the worst defeats of his career when he was sent by Admiral Jervis to attack Tenerife, in the Canary Islands, in July 1797.

Nelson planned the operation carefully but all his careful preparations were frustrated by the one factor for which he could not plan – the weather. His landing force was prevented from reaching their objective by contrary winds and currents and, when they did manage to get ashore, the well-organized Spanish defenders had taken up strong defensive positions and could not be dislodged.

At this point, Nelson received intelligence that the Spanish had very few professional soldiers and were in a state of disarray and confusion. At a council of war with all his captains, he was urged to attack again and needed little persuasion.

RIGHT: Nelson wounded by Richard Westall. A heroic version of the scene painted in 1809 for the 'official' biography by Clarke and M'Arthur. The reality was far less poised and more confused.

GENERAL ANTONIO GUTIÉRREZ
1729–1799

Nelson's opponent at Tenerife was a distinguished and experienced regular soldier. Although Gutiérrez had fewer than 1,500 men, many of them inexperienced volunteers, he deployed them skilfully and beat off Nelson's battle-hardened professionals. After his victory, he then behaved with honour and humanity, offering food and drink to the exhausted attackers and ordering that the British wounded should be treated in the town's hospital.

Horatio Nelson

ABOVE: *One of Nelson's early attempts at signing his name using his left hand.*

The new attack was a disaster that lost Nelson almost a quarter of his force in killed and wounded. As the British sailors and Royal Marines stormed the town jetty and citadel, they were cut down by concentrated fire – including Nelson himself whose upper right arm was shattered by a musket ball. A few small parties managed to struggle ashore and barricaded themselves in a monastery. But they were surrounded and cut off from their comrades and eventually agreed to surrender.

Luckily for Nelson, his stepson, Josiah Nisbet, was at his side in the boat and saved his life. He staunched the flow of blood from the dangerous wound and then managed to get him back to his flagship, where the arm was amputated.

Not unnaturally, Nelson was very depressed – both by the large number of casualties and by the blow to his own future prospects. As he wrote in a letter to Jervis, '… a left-handed admiral will never again be considered as useful.'

Jervis, recently created Earl St Vincent as a reward for his victory, was sympathetic and sent Nelson home to Britain to recover. The arm took a long time to heal but eventually Nelson woke after an unusually sound sleep to find that the pain had suddenly disappeared.

The loss of his arm involved changes in Nelson's life – most obviously the switch to left-handed writing. There were alterations to his clothes: the empty sleeve itself, pinned across his chest; specially shortened right-arm sleeves for his shirts; breeches, stockings and shoes instead of boots.

BELOW: *Nelson's 'kni-fork'. After the loss of his arm at Tenerife, Nelson had to learn how to live with one hand. This special piece of cutlery was designed so that he could cut up his own food.*

The Nile Campaign

ABOVE: *The opening stages of the battle by Nicholas Pocock. As the sun sets, HMS* Goliath *rounds the head of the French line to attack on the inshore side.*

REJOINING ADMIRAL LORD St Vincent's fleet in May 1798, Nelson was immediately detached into the Mediterranean with 14 battleships, commanded by some of the most experienced captains of the fleet. Their mission was to find and destroy a large French expeditionary force, known to be at large, under the overall command of General Napoleon Bonaparte.

After only a year as an admiral, and aged only 39, Nelson now found himself with a level of responsibility that would have taxed an older and more experienced man. He rose to the challenge superbly, tracking the French fleet down in Egypt after a long and frustrating chase and destroying them at anchor in Aboukir Bay, to the east of Alexandria, on 1 August 1798. It was one of the most ferocious and decisive naval battles of the sailing era. Nelson's battle plans had been agreed with his captains some time before. As a result, having made his decision to attack at once, even though night was falling, he was able to leave the detailed conduct of the action to his subordinates.

As the British fleet sailed headlong into Aboukir Bay, Captain Foley in the leading ship HMS *Goliath* noticed that the French had left enough room at the head of their line for him to round their van and attack on the landward side. His bold initiative was followed by the ships astern of him until Nelson, arriving in his flagship HMS *Vanguard*, began a second attack on the seaward side. So, right at the outset, the French van was overwhelmed, crushed on both sides by superior numbers and firepower. And, since the wind was blowing directly down their line, the rearmost ships were unable to do anything to help their comrades and were forced to wait helplessly as the battle rolled towards them. Eventually 11 out of the 13 French battleships were captured or destroyed, including the massive flagship *L'Orient*, which blew up at the height of the battle.

RIGHT: The Hero of the Nile': *James Gilray pokes fun at Nelson's honours for the battle which, he suggests, are weighing him down.*

LEFT: *The dress sword presented to Nelson by the City of London to commemorate the Battle of the Nile.*

Nelson was wounded when a piece of shrapnel struck him on the forehead causing a flap of skin to fall over his good eye. Blinded with blood, he at first thought it was mortal and collapsed into his flag captain Berry's arms saying, 'I am killed. Remember me to my wife.'

The Battle of the Nile is now generally regarded as Nelson's most decisive victory, surpassing even Trafalgar. And Nelson became an international celebrity almost overnight. For the rest of his life, he was known as 'The Hero of the Nile'.

ABOVE: *Nelson's signature after he had been made a Baron.*

ABOVE: *The destruction of L'Orient. As the battle reaches its height at about 10.00 p.m., the French flagship erupts in a shattering series of explosions.*

VICE ADMIRAL PIERRE DE VILLENEUVE
1763–1806

Villeneuve was twice opposed to Nelson. At the Nile he commanded the French rear and managed to escape from the destruction with two battleships. At Trafalgar, in 1805, he was in command of the Combined Fleet. Captured and taken to England, he was allowed to witness Nelson's funeral, but, only days after his return to France, he was found dead. The official verdict was suicide but the suspicion has always lurked that he was assassinated on Napoleon's orders.

Naples and Emma Hamilton
1798–1800

Following the Battle of the Nile, Nelson went to Naples to recover from his wound. He stayed with his friends, the British Envoy, Sir William Hamilton, and his beautiful wife, Emma. It was meant to be a short visit but, in the end, Nelson's close involvement with Naples lasted nearly two years. His actions there were controversial at the time and have remained controversial ever since.

He became caught up in Neapolitan affairs and gradually began to neglect his wider command. When the French occupied Naples and established a republic there, he helped the king to recover his throne in June 1799, so becoming directly involved in a very bloody and vicious civil war. He was personally implicated in some ugly incidents, such as the trial and summary execution of one of the republican leaders, Commodore Franceso Carraciolo, and the surrender for brutal execution of a number of other key Neapolitan revolutionaries. The debate about Nelson's complicity in these atrocities, and whether

LEFT: *Sir William Hamilton. A miniature by Charles Grignon which shows Sir William as the cultured connoisseur and diplomat.*

or not he should be held responsible for them, has continued to this day.

At the same time, he fell in love with Emma Hamilton. She nursed him tenderly when he first arrived in Naples, sick and shaken with his head wound. And she was at his side throughout the events of 1799 when he was wrestling with the complexities of Neapolitan politics. In such an intense atmosphere it was, perhaps, not surprising that two such impetuous and impulsively affectionate people should become close friends, and then lovers.

BELOW: *Nelson's fleet at anchor in the Bay of Naples, by the Neapolitan artist, Giacomo Guardi.*

LEFT: *Nelson's sash and badge as a Knight of the Neapolitan Order of St Ferdinand and Merit.*

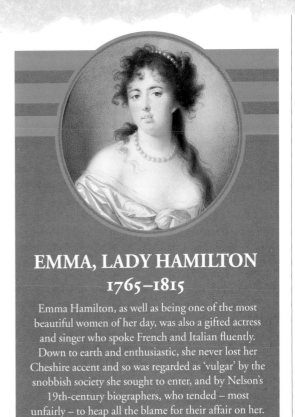

EMMA, LADY HAMILTON
1765–1815

Emma Hamilton, as well as being one of the most beautiful women of her day, was also a gifted actress and singer who spoke French and Italian fluently. Down to earth and enthusiastic, she never lost her Cheshire accent and so was regarded as 'vulgar' by the snobbish society she sought to enter, and by Nelson's 19th-century biographers, who tended – most unfairly – to heap all the blame for their affair on her. Her last years were unhappy, even tragic, with a slow descent into debt, drunkenness and death.

What is surprising is that they did so little to hide it. Modern commentators have suggested that they probably did not start a physical relationship until late in 1799 – but long before then, their public behaviour had already made them a rich source of gossip and scandal.

As for Sir William Hamilton: in the past he has been written off as a foolish old cuckold. However it is now clear that he knew what was happening but was content to ignore the affair, in order to retain the companionship of his wife and the friendship of a man he regarded as a son. In his will he left Nelson a miniature of Emma '… in token of the great regard I have for His Lordship, the most virtuous, loyal and truly brave character I ever met with. God bless him – and shame fall on those who do not say, Amen.'

ABOVE: *Nelson's signature after he had been created Duke of Bronte by the King of Naples.*

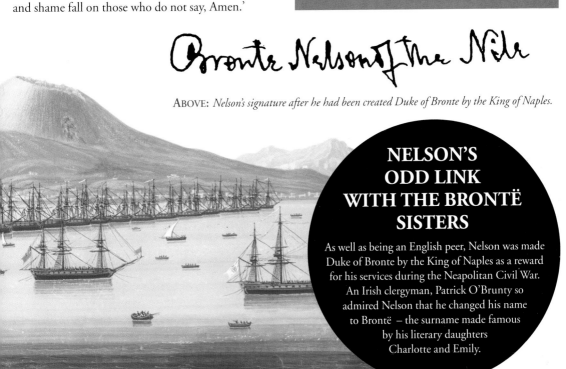

NELSON'S ODD LINK WITH THE BRONTË SISTERS

As well as being an English peer, Nelson was made Duke of Bronte by the King of Naples as a reward for his services during the Neapolitan Civil War. An Irish clergyman, Patrick O'Brunty so admired Nelson that he changed his name to Brontë – the surname made famous by his literary daughters Charlotte and Emily.

Fanny, Emma and Horatia

1800–1801

IN JULY 1800, Nelson and Hamilton were recalled home – both, to some extent, in disgrace. With Emma, they set off through the German states on what quickly became a triumphal progress. Wherever they went there were special ceremonies, and princes and people alike crowded to see the Hero of the Nile. As a result, they stopped so many times en route that a journey they could have expected to make in a few weeks, in fact took three and a half months.

The rumours about Nelson and Emma's affair had preceded them and Fanny Nelson had of course heard

ABOVE: *Frances, Lady Nelson. This watercolour by Henry Edridge, painted in about 1807, captures Fanny's quiet genteel beauty and commemorates her undying devotion to her wayward husband.*

them. It appears that Nelson genuinely believed that his wife would be prepared to be as complacent as Sir William, so that the liaison with Emma could continue. But, although she was bewildered and upset by the breakdown of her marriage, Fanny had her own brand of quiet and dignified courage, against which Nelson's ruthless eagerness beat in vain. In the end, he was forced to choose between his wife and his lover, a decision that clearly wracked him with guilt.

However, Emma had one great advantage over Fanny for, by then, she knew that she was pregnant. The prospect of a child of his own at last obviously

NELSON'S MASS

When Nelson and the Hamiltons visited Vienna in 1800, they met the famous Austrian composer Haydn. One of his great masses was performed in their honour, the *Missa in angustiis* (Mass in straightened times). Since then, it has always been known as 'The Nelson Mass'.

ABOVE: *Dido in Despair by Gilray, shows cruelly how Nelson and Emma's relationship had become a public scandal.*

ABOVE: *Emma, Lady Hamilton. This oil painting, painted in Dresden in 1800 by Johann Schmidt, hung in Nelson's cabin in HMS* Victory. *He called it his 'guardian angel'.*

decided Nelson and the separation from Fanny that followed was cruelly decisive – and so swift that for a while she could not believe it had happened. She poured out her bewilderment, and her longing to win her husband back, in a moving series of letters to one of Nelson's friends, Alexander Davison, that have only recently been discovered. But her husband was relentless and, having made a generous financial provision for her, cut her out of his life and refused to see her, or even to communicate with her, again.

In early 1801, Nelson was summoned to serve at sea once more with the Channel Fleet. He was desperately unhappy at being separated from Emma, and his letters, which he wrote to her almost daily, reflect his emotional instability at this time. Worry about her pregnancy was followed by wild exhilaration when she gave birth to a daughter, Horatia. The child's existence had to be concealed and the couple devised an elaborate charade so that they could write to each other openly about her. They invented a sailor on board Nelson's ship by the name of Thompson who had a pregnant wife that was being looked after by Emma. Nelson then wrote letters to 'Mrs Thompson' apparently on the sailor's behalf passing on tender messages of love to her and the infant.

HORATIA NELSON
1801–1881

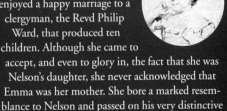

Nelson and Emma's daughter Horatia lived to 80, having enjoyed a happy marriage to a clergyman, the Revd Philip Ward, that produced ten children. Although she came to accept, and even to glory in, the fact that she was Nelson's daughter, she never acknowledged that Emma was her mother. She bore a marked resemblance to Nelson and passed on his very distinctive nose to her descendants.

The Battle of Copenhagen
2 APRIL 1801

IN EARLY 1801, the Baltic states formed themselves into an 'Armed Neutrality of the North' and placed an embargo on British ships. In response, a fleet was sent to the Baltic under the overall command of Admiral Sir Hyde Parker, with Nelson as his second.

Negotiations with Denmark failed and Parker handed over the direction of offensive operations to his subordinate. The Danes had placed a defensive line of hulks and floating batteries in front of Copenhagen, to keep any attacking force out of bombardment range of the city. This had to be subdued – a task made more difficult by the shoals and forts protecting the flanks of the floating line.

Nelson was at his charismatic best, filling everyone with confidence, drawing up detailed plans to deal with the Danish line and then, finally, dining with some of his key subordinates to brief them and infuse them with his fighting spirit.

The ensuing British victory was very much due to Nelson's determination and refusal to be discouraged by mishaps. In the opening moments of the battle he lost a quarter of his attacking force, when three of his ships got into difficulties with the shoals. He then found that the Danish resistance was stronger, and more prolonged, than expected. So the battle dragged on for longer than planned, causing Parker, watching nervously from a distance, to send a signal ordering Nelson to withdraw. Famously, Nelson claimed he could not see the signal and fought on.

About an hour later, sensing that the Danish line was beginning to give way, he sent a message to the Danish Crown Prince offering a truce. By the time the Crown Prince received Nelson's letter, the centre of the Danish line had collapsed and the way was open for a British bombardment. So he agreed to Nelson's suggestion and the battle ended.

Having begun negotiations, Nelson was encouraged by Parker to continue them. The Danes were on the point of agreeing to an armistice when news arrived that Tsar Paul of Russia, the main architect of the Armed Neutrality, had been assassinated. Denmark therefore felt able to withdraw from a confrontation with Britain that had never been popular.

When news of the battle reached Britain, Parker was recalled and Nelson was appointed commander-in-chief. It was an important turning point in his career, when he showed that he was not just a brilliant fighting admiral but a skilled administrator and diplomat as well.

RIGHT: *The seal that Nelson used to close up his letter to the Danish Crown Prince offering a cease-fire.*

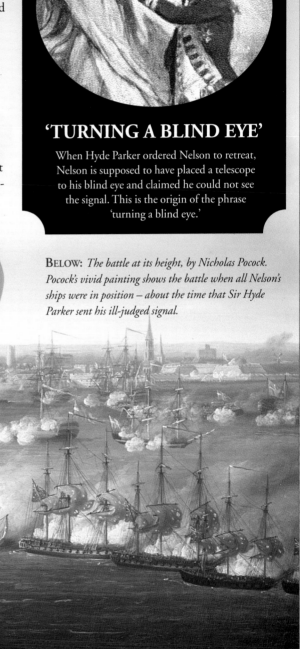

'TURNING A BLIND EYE'

When Hyde Parker ordered Nelson to retreat, Nelson is supposed to have placed a telescope to his blind eye and claimed he could not see the signal. This is the origin of the phrase 'turning a blind eye.'

BELOW: *The battle at its height, by Nicholas Pocock. Pocock's vivid painting shows the battle when all Nelson's ships were in position – about the time that Sir Hyde Parker sent his ill-judged signal.*

The Channel
and Merton
1801–1803

NELSON RETURNED TO Britain in early July 1801 to find the country in the grip of an invasion scare. So he was appointed commander-in-chief of a large fleet of small vessels in the Channel, given the specific task of defending the south coast and the Thames estuary and attacking and destroying the French invasion forces. The move was essentially a public relations exercise, intended to calm public fears by placing the Hero of the Nile in the front line.

ABOVE: John Bull taking a luncheon, *by Gilray. Nelson is shown surrounded by other naval heroes such as Howe, Duncan and St Vincent – but already he is the foremost.*

Nelson quickly realised that the invasion threat was a sham. He made one major attempt to attack the French forces in their harbours, at Boulogne on 15 August, but his opponent, Admiral Louis de Latouche Tréville, was an experienced commander who had studied Nelson's methods and made careful preparations to counter them. As a result, the British attack was repulsed with heavy casualties.

As rumours of approaching peace with France began to circulate in early September 1801, Nelson

pleaded to be allowed to relinquish his command – but his requests were firmly turned down. Eventually, however, at the end of October, the peace negotiations had reached a point where the Government at last felt able to release him and he went ashore to join the Hamiltons.

While Nelson had been at sea, Emma had found a house for him with a small estate attached at Merton, then a small village in Surrey. Despite a very bad surveyor's report, he purchased it with the help of a loan from his friend and agent Alexander Davison. For the next 18 months, he and the Hamiltons often lived there together in a curious, but obviously very amicable, ménage à trois. It was a happy period of quiet retirement, broken only by visits to London,

NELSON'S LARGEST COMMAND

Nelson had over 100 vessels of varying sizes in his fleet in the Channel in the summer of 1801. It was by far the largest force he ever commanded – for example, at Trafalgar he commanded only 33 ships.

where he took part in debates in the House of Lords and, in the summer of 1802, by a protracted tour of South Wales and the Midlands. Planned as a private holiday, it quickly turned into a triumphant progress, showing Nelson at first hand just how popular he was with the ordinary people of Britain.

That popularity was now manifesting itself in a flood of Nelson commemorative material. Nelson's rise to fame coincided with the rise of the cheap press and with the start of mass production of popular goods. So the papers recorded all his movements and carried stories about him and his battles, while his image appeared in every possible medium – from prints and caricatures to ceramics and glassware. As a result, he became instantly recognizable and wherever he went a crowd was sure to gather. He was, to some extent, the first 'pop hero'.

RIGHT AND BELOW:
Nelson commemorative items; Nelson was a popular hero in his own lifetime and cheap souvenirs such as these were best sellers.

LOUIS DE LATOUCHE TRÉVILLE
(1745–1804)

Latouche was one of the most effective French admirals of the Napoleonic period and the only one who could claim he had defeated Nelson. He commanded the French flotilla at Boulogne in 1801, repulsing Nelson's determined and well-planned attack. Later, in 1804, he commanded the French fleet at Toulon but died before he and Nelson could encounter each other. What might have happened had he commanded the French fleet at Trafalgar?

The Mediterranean Command

MAY 1803 – AUGUST 1805

WHEN WAR WITH France broke out again in May 1803, Nelson was given his most prestigious appointment – the command of the Mediterranean Fleet.

The next two years were a remarkable climax to his career. He proved an excellent administrator – keeping his ships afloat and in fighting trim without any dockyard refits and his men happy, healthy and well fed. Nelson ran a most efficient intelligence service, gathering information from all the corners of his command. He also displayed a sure touch as diplomat in his dealings with the rulers of the many different

ABOVE: *Nelson at his desk in HMS* Victory. *All the furnishings and belongings in this posthumous portrait by Charles Lucy were copied directly from Nelson's own possessions.*

countries within his area of interest. With Emma, he appears to have achieved a serenity that was lacking from the earlier years of their relationship. His letters to her were calmer, even mundane, with none of the jealous anguish of the ones he had written in early 1801. Now he wrote to her as if they were a married couple, with gossip about mutual friends, instructions about building projects at Merton and plans for Horatia's future.

Nelson still longed to beat the French one more time. Indeed, instead of blockading them closely in harbour, he constantly tempted them to come out by keeping the main body of his force well out of sight of land. The risk was, of course, that they might be able to escape without his seeing them –

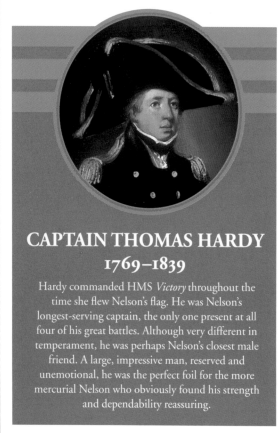

CAPTAIN THOMAS HARDY
1769–1839

Hardy commanded HMS *Victory* throughout the time she flew Nelson's flag. He was Nelson's longest-serving captain, the only one present at all four of his great battles. Although very different in temperament, he was perhaps Nelson's closest male friend. A large, impressive man, reserved and unemotional, he was the perfect foil for the more mercurial Nelson who obviously found his strength and dependability reassuring.

ABOVE: *The Great Cabin of HMS* Victory. *In the foreground is the dining cabin where Nelson entertained his officers; in the background the day cabin where he worked with his secretaries.*

which is exactly what happened twice in 1805. In January the French admiral, Pierre de Villeneuve, managed to elude Nelson's watching frigates but was forced to return to port after encountering a heavy storm. The following March he got clean away to the West Indies at the start of the grand campaign by which Napoleon hoped to unite his fleets with those of the Spanish and bring them as a single, large force to the Channel to cover an invasion of Britain. Nelson chased after them, and succeeded in driving them back to European waters before they could do much damage to the rich British possessions. Then he returned home to Britain for a rest, arriving back at Portsmouth on 19 August 1805.

He arrived to find himself the man of the moment. Politicians, from Prime Minister William Pitt down, wanted to consult him and ask his advice, and whenever he appeared on the streets of London he was surrounded by cheering crowds. As he himself remarked ruefully: 'I am now set up for a conjurer.'

LEFT: *The figurehead of* Victory *as it is today and was when Nelson sailed in her. The original, replaced in an 1801–3 refit, was more ornate.*

'KISS ME HARDY'

As he lay dying below decks in *Victory*, Nelson asked Hardy to kiss him. This touching request, so in keeping with Nelson's character and the spirit of his times, was misunderstood by later generations who ludicrously suggested that what he had said was 'Kismet' (Turkish for 'fate'). However, contemporary accounts agree that the kiss was asked for – and that Hardy kissed Nelson twice, first on the cheek and then on the forehead.

Trafalgar

21 OCTOBER 1805

THE COMBINED FRENCH and Spanish fleets had taken refuge in Cádiz and the Admiralty began assembling a fleet to deal with them. The command was offered to Nelson as a matter of course. Before he left Merton, he went with Emma to the parish church, where they took private communion and exchanged rings in a quasi-marriage service. They had had only 25 days together.

He arrived off Cádiz on 28 September. Only a handful of the captains had served with him before and so he had to build a new band of brothers in a few days. The next day, his 47th birthday, he held a dinner party in the *Victory* at which he explained his plan for defeating the enemy, 'The Nelson Touch', as he called it. As at the Nile and Copenhagen, his aim was to bring overwhelming force to bear on one part of the enemy's line, to crush it as quickly as possible. To achieve this, he aimed to attack in two divisions, splitting his opponents' line into three segments. And, in a single phrase, he summed up his leadership ethos, '… in case signals can neither be seen or perfectly understood, no captain can do very wrong if he places his ship alongside that of an enemy.' The man who had seized the initiative at Cape St Vincent was now empowering his subordinates to do the same.

ABOVE: *'England Expects'. Thomas Davidson shows Nelson talking to Captains Hardy and Blackwood as the signalmen behind him hoist the flags spelling out his famous message.*

ABOVE: *The battle at its height c.3.00 p.m. by Thomas Luny, painted in 1807. The* Victory *(centre) is partly obscured by smoke and is flying Nelson's last signal for 'Close Action'.*

The Franco-Spanish fleet emerged from Cádiz on 19 October 1805, heading south. Napoleon had now started a new campaign against Austria and had ordered the French admiral, Villeneuve, to sail into the Mediterranean in support. Nelson shadowed them until they were well clear of harbour and then, on the morning of 21 October, turned to attack.

The battle unfolded very much as he had planned. One British division, under Vice Admiral Cuthbert Collingwood, enveloped the allied rear, crushing it with superior gunfire, while another under Nelson smashed through the centre of the allied line, cutting it in two and preventing the van from helping their

LEFT: *The spot where Nelson fell on HMS Victory's quarterdeck is marked with a brass plaque. A wreath is placed there every year on Trafalgar Day.*

Nelson & Bronte, oct. 20

ABOVE: *Nelson's signature on one of the last letters he ever wrote.*

comrades. Having led the way through a hail of shot, the *Victory* became entangled with a smaller French battleship, the *Redoutable*, and it was from her rigging that the bullet was fired which struck Nelson at about 1.15 p.m., as he was pacing the quarterdeck with Captain Thomas Hardy. Carried down to the cockpit below the *Victory*'s waterline, where the wounded were treated in comparative safety, he lingered, in great pain, long enough to learn that he had won a decisive victory. His last words were, 'Thank God I have done my duty.'

Of the 33 French and Spanish ships that had begun the battle, 18 had been either captured or destroyed, four escaped only to be captured a fortnight later at the Battle of Cape Ortegal and only 11 managed to struggle back into Cádiz.

ABOVE: The Death of Nelson, *by Arthur Devis. Nelson prepares to take leave of Hardy (standing) as Chaplain Scott (left) and Surgeon Beatty attend to him.*

The Immortal Memory

REJOICING AT THE remarkable victory at Trafalgar was overshadowed by grief at the loss of Nelson. Midshipman Joseph Woollnough of HMS *Agamemnon* recorded that when his comrades heard the news, 'A stranger might have supposed from the gloom that spread among them that they had been beaten instead of being conquerors.'

When the news reached Britain, there was similar mixed reaction. As Robert Southey, the Poet Laureate, later recalled in his *Life of Nelson*, published in 1813, 'The victory of Trafalgar was celebrated, indeed, with the usual forms of rejoicing, but they were without joy.' Nelson's body was brought home and lay in state in the Painted Hall in Greenwich Hospital before being transported to London in an elaborate river procession. It was then taken to St Paul's Cathedral where, after a spectacular funeral service, it was finally laid to rest in the crypt, immediately beneath the great dome.

Nelson's life and death were celebrated in a surge of heroic paintings, statues, poetry and popular art. Anything that had belonged to him was preserved as a sacred relic – from the bullet that killed him and the blood-stained coat he was wearing at Trafalgar to ordinary items such as his shoe buckles and handkerchiefs. Most macabre of all, his hair was cut off and distributed amongst his friends.

ABOVE: *Nelson's funeral procession on the River Thames. The body is in the third barge from the left under a canopy.*

BELOW: *The funeral car bearing Nelson's body arrives at St Paul's Cathedral, watched by a vast crowd.*

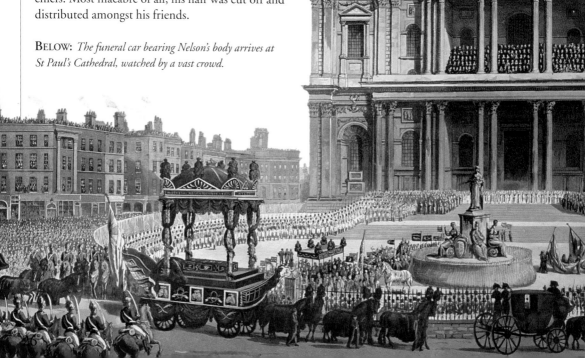